TRANQUILITY THROUGH
Mindfulness

Robert Leihy

ISBN: Softcover   978-1-7960-2371-8
         EBook   978-1-7960-2372-5

Print information available on the last page

Rev. date: 03/26/2019

To order additional copies of this book, contact:
Xlibris
1-888-795-4274
www.Xlibris.com
Orders@Xlibris.com

TRANQUILITY THROUGH Mindfulness

Relaxation

AFTER A SUCCESSFUL SPA TREATMENT, A PERSON COULD BE LEFT IN NEAR-PERFECT RELAXATION.   A RELAXED PERSON WOULD FEEL CONTENTED PHYSICALLY AND WOULD BE AT PEACE WITH THE WORLD AND WITH HIMSELF. HE WOULD BE SATISFIED AND CONTENT IN THE HERE-AND-NOW. HE WOULD FEEL NO NEEDS OR DESIRES. AT THE SAME TIME, HE WOULD CONTINUE TO PERCEIVE THE WORLD WITH RELAXED ALERTNESS AND NORMAL MENTAL ACUITY. STRESSES WOULD SEEM TO BE AT A DISTANCE FOR THE TIME BEING. HE WOULD BE LIVING IN A "BUBBLE" OF PEACE. THIS IDEAL OF THIS STATE OF BEING COULD ALSO BE CALLED THE "MINDFUL" STATE OR THE "ENLIGHTENED" STATE.

THE WORLD DOES NOT CHANGE DURING A SPA TREATMENT, BUT INSTEAD THE CONCEPTUAL PERSPECTIVE OF IT DOES.

THE MINDFULNESS PHILOSOPHY AND OTHERS POINT OUT THAT THIS SAME STATE CAN ALSO BE APPROACHED AND REACHED NATURALLY WITH PRACTICE ALONE. ALSO, IT CAN BE QUITE INDEPENDENT OF CURRENT OUTSIDE CIRCUMSTANCES.   IT CAN BRING GREATER TRANQUILITY TO DAILY LIFE.

SINCE OUR EXISTENCE PRESENTS US WITH A COMPLEX NETWORK OF POSITIVES AND NEGATIVES, AN APPROPRIATE WORLDVIEW, DISCUSSED LATER, WOULD BE NECESSARY TO MAINTAIN THE MINDFUL PERSPECTIVE CONTINUOUSLY.

THE SEARCH FOR WELL-BEING IS PART OF THE SURVIVAL INSTINCT, SO BY ITSELF IT INCURS NO GUILT.

SINCE STRESS IS FELT AND EXPRESSED EXCLUSIVELY IN MUSCLE TENSIONS, INCREASED RELAXATION OF THE BODY REDUCES STRESS REACTIONS. SUCH RELAXATION IS A REFUGE FROM STRESS AND FOR THIS REASON ALONE IS WORTH PRACTICING.

THE MINDFULNESS PHILOSOPHY POINTS OUT THAT ALTHOUGH A A PHYSICAL OR MENTAL STRESSOR CAN EVOKE MUSCLE TENSION IN THE BODY, THE BODY CAN BE TRAINED TO AUTOMATICALLY REACT TO STRESS SITUATIONS WITH A RELAXATION RESPONSE INSTEAD. ONE CAN PRACTICE LETTING GO INSTEAD OF TIGHTENING UP WHEN STRESSFUL SITUATIONS TAKE PLACE. HE WILL RETAIN HIS RATIONALITY AND OBJECTIVITY AT THE SAME TIME, THUS SUBDUING THE FIGHT-OR-FLIGHT EMOTIONS THAT ARISE FROM THE SURVIVAL INSTINCT. SOME CALL IT "GRACE UNDER FIRE"..

AS RELAXATION BECOMES A MORE HABITUAL AUTOMATIC RESPONSE, ONE STAYS MORE TRANQUIL DURING THE UPS AND DOWNS OF THE DAY WITHOUT EVEN THINKING ABOUT IT. THE MIND STILL PERCEIVES THE STRESS, BUT RELAXATION BECOMES THE CONDITIONED RESPONSE.

RELAXATION PRACTICE IS THE ROYAL ROAD TO CONTENTMENT. IT IS A SINGLE OBSERVABLE PATH.   ONE CAN FEEL IT AND CHANGE HIS POSITION ON IT.

STRESS AND RELAXATION ARE OPPOSITE ENDS OF THE SAME CONTINUUM. MORE OF ONE MEANS LESS OF THE OTHER.

PHILOSOPHIES AND RELIGIONS THAT PROPOSE THE SAME SORTS OF EXPERIENCES ARE CONCEPTUALLY MORE SWEEPING AND DETAILED IN NATURE THAN IS THE SINGLE PATH OF RELAXATION.

NEGATIVES CAN STILL BE THOUGHT ABOUT AND ANALYZED WHEN RELAXED, BUT THE NEGATIVE EMOTIONAL COMPONENT IS REDUCED OR NOT PRESENT AT ALL. OBJECTIVE ANALYSIS OF NEGATIVES WHILE RELAXED CAN BE PRODUCTIVE AND SATISFYING.

TO PRACTICE RELAXATION, ONE CAN LET GO A LITTLE MORE AT THE END OF EACH EXHALATION. SOFT BREATHING HELPS BECAUSE THE BREATHING MUSCLES ARE VERY SENSITIVE TO BOTH MENTAL AND PHYSICAL STRESS. ONE CANNOT STRIVE FOR RELAXATION BECAUSE STRIVING IS TENSION. A MENTAL CONCEPT AND IMAGE OF ONESELF AT PERFECT PEACE IS A GOOD ADDITION TO ONE'S PERSONAL LIBRARY OF MENTAL CONCEPTS.

Worldview

TO PRACTICE RELAXATION, ONE CAN LET GO A LITTLE MORE AT THE END OF EACH EXHALATION. SOFT BREATHING HELPS BECAUSE THE BREATHING MUSCLES ARE VERY SENSITIVE TO BOTH MENTAL AND PHYSICAL STRESS. ONE CANNOT STRIVE FOR RELAXATION BECAUSE STRIVING IS TENSION. A MENTAL CONCEPT AND IMAGE OF ONESELF AT PERFECT PEACE IS A GOOD ADDITION TO ONE'S PERSONAL LIBRARY OF MENTAL CONCEPTS.

A POSITIVE AND VALID WORLDVIEW THAT ACCOMMODATES ALL OR MOST WORLDLY CIRCUMSTANCES IS NECESSARY IN ORDER TO MAINTAIN A MINDFUL OUTLOOK AND STATE OF BEING DAY BY DAY.

AN APPROPRIATE, VALID, AND POPULAR WORLDVIEW STARTS WITH THE FACT THAT THE PHYSICAL UNIVERSE IS MADE ENTIRELY OF ATOMS.

WITHOUT AN ORGANIZING PRINCIPLE AT WORK, THE ATOMS WOULD BE SCATTERED RANDOMLY. INSTEAD, THE ATOMS ARE HIGHLY ORGANIZED INTO STRUCTURES SUCH AS THE HUMAN BODY, THE HUMAN BRAIN, THE TABLES AND THE CHAIRS, AND EVEN THE AIR THAT WE BREATHE. OUR EXISTENCE IS ORGANIZED ATOMS.

A MYSTERIOUS UNSEEN HIGHER POWER CONTINUOUSLY PLACES, MOVES, AND ORGANIZES ALL OF THE ATOMS AT ONCE TO PRODUCE OUR EVER-CHANGING EXISTENCE, AS WE KNOW IT.

IF WE LOOK AT A CITY BLOCK OR A FOREST, WE KNOW FOR SURE WE DID NOT ORGANIZE THE ATOMS TO CREATE THEM. SOMETHING ELSE DID.

IF THE HIGHER POWER DID NOT ORGANIZE ALL OF THE ATOMS, THERE WOULD BE "HOLES" FOUND IN EXISTENCE OCCUPIED BY NOTHING BUT RANDOM ATOMS. IN ADDITION, THE HIGHER POWER MUST EVEN ORGANIZE THE ATOMS OF OUR BRAINS IN SUCH A WAY AS TO CONTINUALLY PRODUCE ALL OF OUR MINDS AND OUR CONTENTS OF CONSCIOUSNESS. THE MIND-BRAIN BOUNDARY IS CERTAINLY A MYSTERY.

THE DALAI LAMA REFERRED TO THE MYSTERY OF THE SOURCE OF THOUGHT WHEN HE ASKED THE QUESTION: "HOW DOES THE BRAIN KNOW WHAT THOUGHT TO THINK NEXT?"

A LOGICAL CONCLUSION TO THIS LINE OF REASONING WOULD BE THAT THE HIGHER POWER, THE ORGANIZER OF THE ATOMS, CREATES ALL OF THE ELEMENTS OF EXISTENCE, EVEN OUR THOUGHTS. 'ALL THE WORLD IS A STAGE AND THE PEOPLE ARE PLAYERS WITH AWARENESS'.

IN ADDITION, THE HIGHER POWER DIRECTS COUNTLESS MENTAL AND PHYSICAL DRAMAS ALL AROUND THE WORLD ALL DAY LONG. BESIDES BEING ALL-PERVADING, ALL-SEEING, ALL-KNOWING, AND ALL-POWERFUL, HE KNOWS AND MANIPULATES ALL DRAMA. IT IS DIFFICULT TO CONCEPTUALIZE A BEING WITH SUCH CAPABILITIES, BUT IT MUST EXIST OTHERWISE WE WOULD NOT BE HERE. THE HUMAN DRAMA IS THE MOST COMPLEX ORGANIZATION OF ATOMS IN THE KNOWN UNIVERSE. AS SUCH, IT COULD BE ASSUMED TO BE ITS HIGHEST KNOWN PURPOSE.

PHRASES IN OUR LANGUAGE CONFIRM OUR GENERAL ACCEPTANCE OF THIS POINT OF VIEW: IT WAS GOD'S WILL, THANK GOD, GOD WILLING, THE LORD MOVES IN STRANGE WAYS, ONLY GOD KNOWS, WHAT WILL BE WILL BE, COME WHAT MAY, ETC.

THE FIRST SUNLIGHT IN WASHINGTON D.C. FALLS ON A PLAQUE ATOP THE WASHINGTON MONUMENT THAT SAYS "PRAISE GOD".

EXISTENCE IS ENTIRELY COHERENT AND CONSISTENT. THERE ARE NO HOLES, OVERLAPS, OR TIME OR DRAMA DISTORTIONS TO BE FOUND IN IT. NATURAL LAWS PRECISELY LIMIT IT AND CONSTRAIN ITS EXPRESSION AND ARE SEEMINGLY ENTIRELY RELIABLE.

IT IS POSSIBLE TO DEFINE ONESELF AS A STAND-ALONE ATOMIC PROCESS EXISTING WITHIN THE LARGER ATOMIC PROCESS THAT MAKES UP HIS SURROUNDINGS. ONE'S SKIN BECOMES THE BOUNDARY BETWEEN THE SELF AND THE REST OF EXISTENCE.

ON THE OTHER HAND, ONE CAN DEFINE HIMSELF AS AN ATOMIC PROCESS COMPLETELY BLENDED INTO AND MOVING ALONG WITH THE SURROUNDING OVERALL ATOMIC PROCESS. HIS SKIN BECOMES A LAYER OF ATOMS THAT INEXTRICABLY JOINS HIM WITH THE REST OF THE ATOMS OF EXISTENCE. THE DROP OF WATER BECOMES THE OCEAN. EACH POINT IF VIEW HAS MANY IMPLICATIONS, AND BOTH ARE VALID. WE REALLY DO LIVE ENTIRELY IN OUR MINDS AND WE RELATE TO THEIR CONTENTS AS REALITIES.   AT THE SAME TIME, ATOMS SEEM TO BE A REALITY AND THEY HAVE TO BE ORGANIZED SOMEHOW TO PRODUCE THE STRUCTURES AND MENTAL EXPERIENCES THAT MAKE UP OUR EXISTENCE.

IN ANY CASE, OUR STREAM OF MENTAL CONSCIOUS IS OUR ONLY EXISTENCE AND IT IS ALL WE HAVE.

EXISTENCE, INCLUDING OURSELVES, CAN BE CONCEPTUALIZED AS MIRACULOUSLY EMERGING FROM AN UNKNOWN SOURCE AND CHANGING SEEMINGLY BY ITSELF MOMENT BY MOMENT. WHY IT TAKES THE PARTICULAR ATOMIC FORM THAT IT DOES, ONLY GOD KNOWS.

OUR PERSONAL EGOS HAVE BEEN DESIGNED BY OUR BRAINS IN
SUCH A WAY THAT IT SEEMS TO US THAT WE HAVE THE FREE WILL
TO CHOOSE OUR ACTIONS AND OUR THOUGHTS. WE CAN
CHOOSE HOW WE AFFECT THE WORLD. WE CAN CHOOSE
THE CONCEPTS THAT WE WISH TO USE IN ORDER TO
EXPLAIN OUR REALITY.

ONE CAN CHOOSE TO LEARN AND DEEPEN THE OVERALL MINDFUL PERSPECTIVE OF THE HERE-AND-NOW WORLD. IT WOULD INCLUDE PLEASURABLE DEEP RELAXATION, ACCEPTANCE OF CURRENT CIRCUMSTANCES, ATTENTIVENESS, ALERTNESS, SUFFICIENT DETACHMENT FROM THE LESS USEFUL DRAMAS THAT UNFOLD IN HIS EXISTENCE, AND A SENSE OF "LETTING GO" AND BEING A PART OF HIS EXPERIENCE. HE CAN "GO WITH THE FLOW" AND "LET THE WORLD GO BY" WITH MINIMAL RESISTANCE OR CLINGING. 'LETTING GO" CAN BE A THIRD APPROACH TO EXISTENCE. AS DANCERS SOMETIME SAY: "LET THE BODY DANCE ITSELF". THE DIFFERENCE IS IN THE CHANGED CONCEPT THAT ONE MOVES FROM A STANDALONE BEING INFLUENCING THE FLOW OF HIS EXISTENCE TO ONE OF BEING AN INTEGRAL PART OF AN EXISTENCE THAT IS BEING CHOREOGRAPHED BY AN EXTERNAL AGENT.

EVEN THOUGH EMERGING EXISTENCE IS A MYSTERY, ONE CAN BE ACCEPTING OF AND CONTENTED WITHIN THE MYSTERY AND STILL MAKE ANY ASSUMPTIONS HE WISHES REGARDING ITS NATURE AND PURPOSE. OVERALL, THE MYSTERY SEEMS TO TAKE CARE OF ITSELF.

IF ONE'S CONCEPT OF BEING A PART OF EVERYTHING BECOMES MORE VIVID, CONCERN ABOUT THE FUTURE DIMINISHES. THE CONCEPT THAT GOD'S WILL PREVAIL TAKES ITS PLACE.   IT IS A STEP TOWARD DEEPER CONTENTMENT TO TRUST A HIGHER POWER. THE EGO LOSES SOME OF ITS URGENT EXCESSIVE FEELINGS OF RESPONSIBILITY FOR THE WAY THINGS TURN OUT. INSTEAD, THE CONCEPT THAT 'T "HIS WILL BE DONE" TENDS TO PREVAIL

PAYING RESPECT TO THE MIRACLE OF EXISTENCE AND TO ITS CREATOR CAN BE A FORM OF A PERSONAL EXPRESSION OF GRATITUDE FOR THE PRIVILEGE OF BEING HERE AS A PART OF THE UNFOLDING MYSTERY.

HAVING THE CONTINUOUS INTENTION OF MAKING POSITIVE CONTRIBUTIONS INTO ONE'S EXISTENCE WHEN OPPORTUNITIES ARISE WILL HELP TO INSURE A GOOD RELATIONSHIP WITH IT AND WILL HELP HIM TO FEEL JUSTIFIED IN HIS BEING HERE. IT WILL HELP TO CREATE A MORE POSITIVE SELF-IMAGE AND HOPEFULLY TO MAKE IT A BETTER WORLD. IT WILL ALSO AVOID THE ACCUMULATION OF PERSONAL GUILT.

AN ABUSIVE LIFESTYLE BRINGS ABOUT FEELINGS OF DEFENSIVENESS AND GUILT. THE WORLD LOOKS HOSTILE TO THESE PEOPLE AND THEY ACT ACCORDINGLY..

IT SEEMS THAT THE QUALITY OF ONE'S CONTRIBUTION TO HIS OUTSIDE WORLD STAYS THERE AND IS EXPECTED TO EVENTUALLY COME BACK IN ONE FORM OR ANOTHER. A LADY I KNEW ONCE SAID "I DESERVE EVERY BAD THING THAT EVER HAPPENED TO ME". THIS APPARENT RELATIONSHIP IS BASED ON THE CONCEPT THAT ONE AND HIS WORLD SHARE THE SAME EXISTENCE. 'THAT ART THOU''.

AS THEE SOW, SO SHALL YE REAP. WHAT GOES AROUND COMES AROUND. WE CAN CHOOSE TO MAKE THIS CYCLE POSITIVE AND CAN PRACTICE DOING SO.

THE EXPERIENCE OF DEEP RELAXATION IN A CONTENTED BODY WITH A MIND AT PEACE IS ABOUT AS GOOD AS IT GETS HERE ON THIS PARTICULAR PLANE OF EXISTENCE.

Printed in the United States
By Bookmasters